Exploring Remembrance Day

Dr Brian Knapp

World history

3000 BC   **2000 BC**   **1000 BC**

Ancient Egyptians (3000–332 BC)

Ancient Greek

1914

June 28: Assassination of Austrian heir to the throne causes the start of the First World War

August 3: Germany declares war on France

August 4: The United Kingdom declares war on Germany

August 7: The first British troops arrive in France

September 5: British and French stop the German advance on Paris

September 13: Troops from South Africa invade German South-West Africa

October 19: The First Battle of Ypres stops the Germans reaching the North Sea along the line of the River Somme. The long stalemate along the Western Front begins

November 2: The United Kingdom begins stopping ships reaching Germany

December 8: Battle of the Falklands. German fleet is defeated by the Royal Navy

December 24–25: An unofficial Christmas truce is declared between large numbers of German and French forces

1915

January 19: First Zeppelin airship raid on Great Britain. Bombs dropped on London

February 4: Germany begins submarine warfare against British ships

February 19: The British and French attack Turkey at Gallipoli

April 22–May 25: The Germans use poison gas for the first time

May 7: The British liner Lusitania is sunk by a German U-boat. It has Americans on board

1916

January 27: Men called up in the United Kingdom

May 31–June 1: Battle of Jutland between Britain's Grand Fleet and Germany's navy. The British stop the Germans getting out of their harbours

July 1: The Battle of the Somme begins

September 15: In the Battle of the Somme the British use tanks for the first time in history

November 18: The Battle of the Somme ends. Huge number of casualties. Stalemate continues

1917

January 16: The Germans send a telegram to Mexico, suggesting the Mexican government fights against the United States. The telegram is decoded by the British and made public. There is great anger at Germany in America

March 8: The British capture Baghdad (Iraq)

April 6: The United States of America declares war on Germany

June 25: First American troops land in France

July 6: Arab rebels led by Lawrence of Arabia seize the Jordanian port of Aqaba

November 7: Russian revolution starts and Russia can no longer fight in the war. It signs a peace treaty with Germany and loses much land

December 11: The Battle of Jerusalem. The British enter the city

1918

August 8: The allies including America begin their long final attack on the Western Front

September 18: The Allies break through the German lines

November 11: Germany signs the Armistice with the allies. End of fighting at 11 am

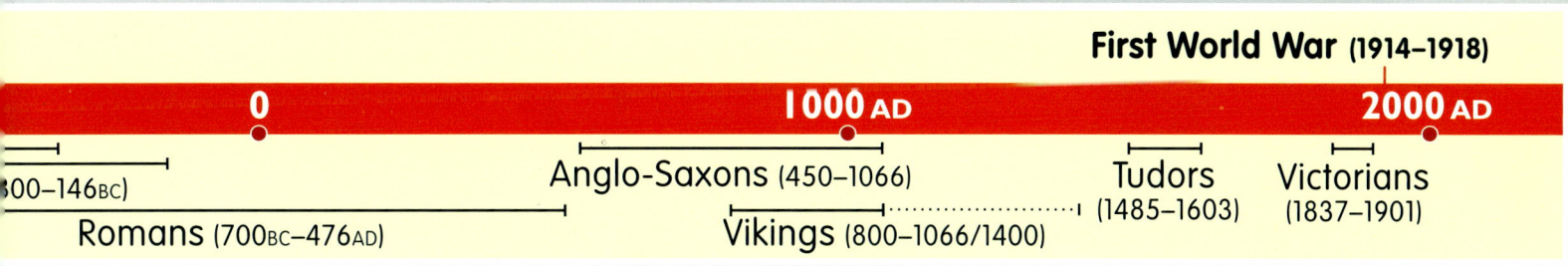

First World War (1914–1918)

| 0 | 1000 AD | 2000 AD |

300–146BC)

Anglo-Saxons (450–1066)

Tudors (1485–1603)

Victorians (1837–1901)

Romans (700BC–476AD)

Vikings (800–1066/1400)

Contents

Look up the **bold** words in the glossary on page 32 of this book.

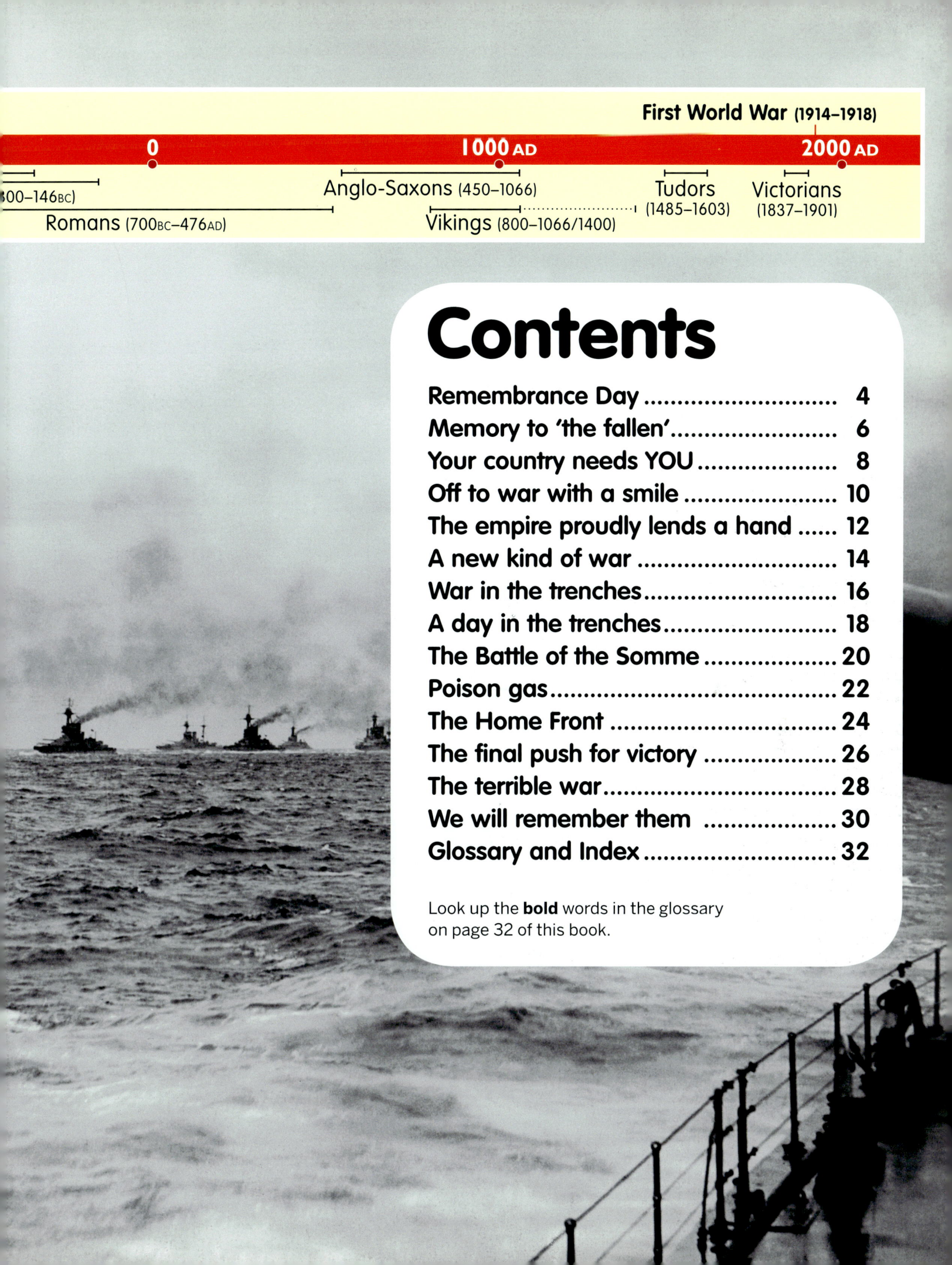

Remembrance Day

This is the story of Remembrance Day, the anniversary of the day near the end of the First World War when fighting stopped between the **Allies** and Germany. It was not the end of the war, but it was the end of the fighting, and the end of the killing.

After four wearying years of fighting, the king at the time, King George V, wanted to make sure we always remembered the war and its suffering. And so, in 1919, a day was set aside for this. We now call it Remembrance Day. It marks the **Armistice** Day close to the end of the First World War. But wars did not stop with the First World War and so it has seemed right to use that day to honour all the troops who have been lost in the wars since that time, including those who have been lost only recently.

There is a silence of two minutes at 11 am on the 11th day of the 11th month. Then, on the Sunday nearest to it, there is a ceremony of laying of wreaths of poppies. Poppies were used as a symbol of the war because they were the first flowers to bloom on the battlefields after the end of the war.

War memorials are places where we can remember the fallen of all wars – and remember to do all in our power to prevent wars from happening again.

Q **What is the purpose of Remembrance Day?**

Memory to 'the fallen'

When people speak of those killed in the wars since the First World War, nearly a century ago, they refer to them as 'the fallen'.

In the First World War millions of soldiers were killed and fell on the battlefields as they fought for four long years. In many cases there was no time to bury the dead. In other cases, the dead were buried in unmarked graves.

After the war was over, nations tried to find as many of these fallen soldiers as possible and give them dignified burials in special war graves.

If you visit northern France even today, the fields of gleaming white graves can still be seen. Only when you see row after row of graves stretching into the distance, can you begin to imagine the losses that war brings.

On Remembrance Day, which was started soon after the First World War ended, we remember all of the fallen soldiers, not just from those terrible days, but from all wars since, right up to the brave soldiers who are still protecting us and our country today in many far-flung corners of the world, just as they did a century ago.

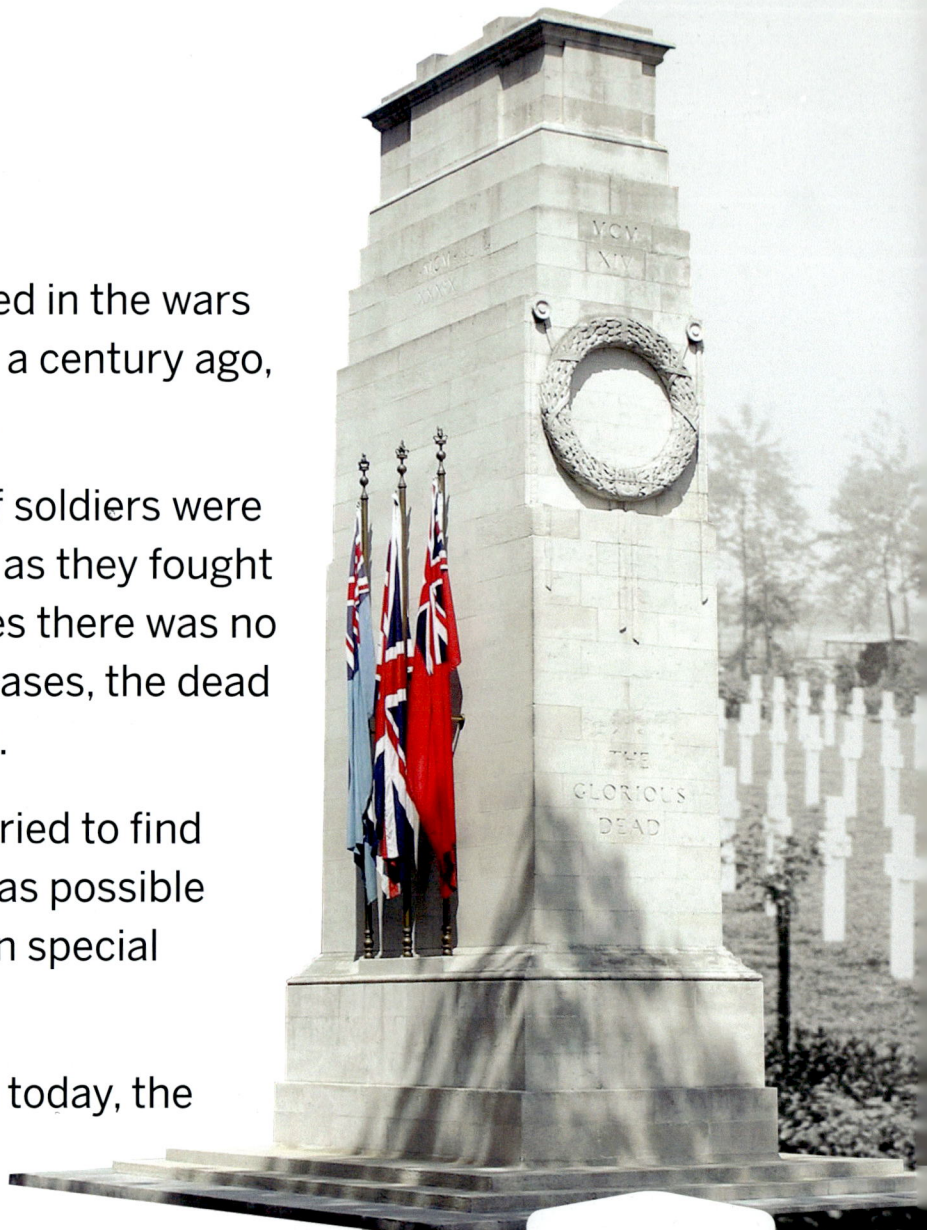

The Cenotaph, London.

This photograph was taken in the 1920s in Flanders, France at the site of some of the fiercest fighting. At this time the graves had only recently been laid out.

Did you know…?

- That the UK National Memorial to all the fallen is the Cenotaph in Whitehall, London.
- That the word Cenotaph means 'empty tomb'.
- That the national tomb for the First World War is in Westminster Abbey and contains the remains of an unknown soldier as a symbol for all the fallen.
- That all uniformed service people salute the Cenotaph as they pass throughout the year.
- That the Queen and all government leaders and representatives of the Commonwealth always attend the Remembrance Day service.
- That the Cenotaph was first built of wood in 1919 and then rebuilt in limestone in 1920.

Q Why do we have a national war memorial?

Your country needs YOU

The First World War (also called WWI and World War I) was caused when a student in Serbia, in Eastern Europe, a long way from Britain, killed the heir to the throne of Austria, also a long way from Britain. So how did Britain and other countries around the world come to be involved?

It was because all of the countries of Europe were linked together by treaties that said if any country was attacked, the other partners in the treaty would come to its aid.

So although the war started far away, within months it involved the whole of Europe.

European countries had colonies around the world, so when their 'mother country' was attacked,

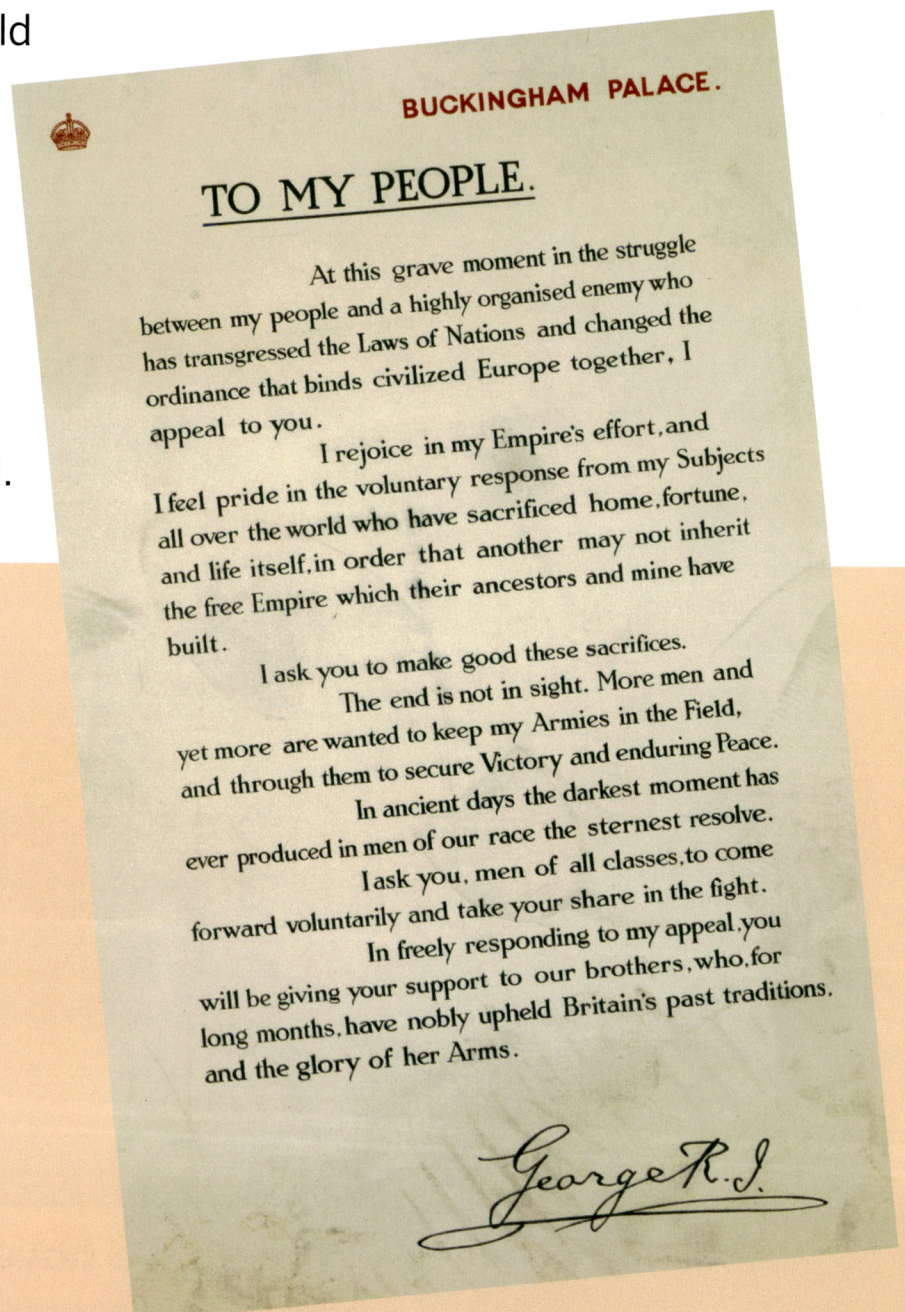

Did you know… ?

- The face on the poster is Lord Kitchener. At the time he was the most successful and popular general in Britain.
- For two years all the soldiers in the war were volunteers.

BUCKINGHAM PALACE.

TO MY PEOPLE.

At this grave moment in the struggle between my people and a highly organised enemy who has transgressed the Laws of Nations and changed the ordinance that binds civilized Europe together, I appeal to you.

I rejoice in my Empire's effort, and I feel pride in the voluntary response from my Subjects all over the world who have sacrificed home, fortune, and life itself, in order that another may not inherit the free Empire which their ancestors and mine have built.

I ask you to make good these sacrifices.

The end is not in sight. More men and yet more are wanted to keep my Armies in the Field, and through them to secure Victory and enduring Peace.

In ancient days the darkest moment has ever produced in men of our race the sternest resolve.

I ask you, men of all classes, to come forward voluntarily and take your share in the fight.

In freely responding to my appeal, you will be giving your support to our brothers, who, for long months, have nobly upheld Britain's past traditions, and the glory of her Arms.

George R.I.

the colonies were soon involved, too.

Britain only had a small army at the start of the war, so it had to find a way of getting men to volunteer. As a result, the king wrote a personal letter, and the government started a poster campaign. You can see the most famous poster here.

"YOUR COUNTRY NEEDS YOU

Q Why do you think this poster worked so well?

Off to war with a smile

The First World War was fought by a country that was still largely 'Victorian'. Everyone had principles of 'honour' and 'duty' of 'sacrifice' and 'military glory '. It was an age of patriots.

No-one questioned the war. They did not have to. They saw war as a matter of honour (the treaties they had with other countries to defend them if attacked). This is why, until January 1916, the British army was almost entirely made of 2.5 million volunteers led by just a few professionals.

It is important to understand this because it is not how everybody feels today. So we must not put what some people say about war today into the minds of people in the past. This was their war, and we should see it as they did or we will not understand what happened.

- Most troops thought the war would be over in a few months without a single shot being fired.
- Many soldiers were under 16 years of age. They falsified their age so they could be part of the 'great adventure'.

Q **Why did people laugh and joke as they went to war?**

War in the trenches

The German army met the British and French armies in northern France. Much of this land is fairly flat, so there is no natural cover where soldiers could protect themselves. Remember that, in this war, most of the troops were on foot. They were taken near to the battlegrounds (which were known as 'the Front') by train and then they walked the rest of the way.

Remember, too, that new weapons, such as the machine gun and big guns that fired '**shells**', had recently been invented. The troops could not survive out in the open against machine-gun fire and shell explosions, so they dug trenches to protect themselves (they 'dug-in').

Once they had dug trenches, they were trapped. Neither side could move forward. This is why the war became a **stalemate**.

The Home Front

The war affected people at home, just as much as on the front line. The effort people made at home was vital. This is why it became known as the Home Front.

As more and more men went off to the Western Front, so the number of men left to work at home got smaller. In some places there were only women, children and the elderly. The exceptions were skilled people, who were needed to help the war effort at home.

Factories still had to produce guns, shells and all the other materials needed for war. Farms still had to produce the food that everyone needed. As there were few men to do these jobs, women had to take their places. Food had to be sent to the troops on the Front, as well, and this was almost more than the country could manage.

Before the war most family women worked only at home. They did not have jobs that brought in wages. Now women had to do jobs that men had done before. It would change Britain for ever.

Q **Why did women have to go to work during the war?**

The final push for victory

By 1917 the Europeans were weary of war. They had fought themselves to a standstill. How were they to end it all?

The answer was to come in the form of public anger in America – a country that had stayed neutral because it was made up of immigrants from all the countries now at war. So it was hard for America to take sides.

Then the Germans started to use submarines to sink ships sailing to Britain. The Americans were not at war, so they believed their ships would be left alone – including ships of other nations carrying Americans.

However, in 1915 a German submarine attacked and sunk a passenger liner called the Lusitania.

More than a thousand people died, including 138 Americans. Americans were shocked, but still nothing happened.

A painting of the sinking of the Lusitania.

The telegram

In February 1917, Britain gave the American government a telegram sent by the Germans asking Mexico to join the war and attack America. The telegram was made public, and instantly the mood in America changed. People now demanded war. On the 6th of April 1917 the United States finally declared war on Germany.

The American forces tipped the balance. They were fresh men, not weary of war. They were extra men – 10,000 more every day. The final push began on the 8th of August 1918. The Germans quickly realised they could not hold out any longer. In September they began to look for a peace treaty. On the 11th of November, Germany signed an Armistice. All fighting stopped at exactly 11am.

American troops throw hand grenades at a German position.

Q **Why did the Americans stay out of the war for so long?**

The terrible war

The First World War was called 'the terrible war', and it was meant to be the 'war to end all wars'. Of course we know it wasn't. It did not even have the most casualties. There were more in the Second World War.

Why, then, was the First World War called the 'terrible war'? Well, it was due to the indescribably ghastly conditions in which soldiers fought – and the fact that no-one in charge seemed to care.

Casualties from the British Empire and the USA
(The numbers serving were much higher than this)

Country	Dead	Wounded	Missing (presumed dead)	Total
Australia	58,150	152,170	-	210,320
Britain	658,700	2,032,150	359,150	3,050,000
Canada	56,500	149,700	-	206,200
Caribbean	1,000	3,000	-	4,000
India	43,200	65,175	5,875	114,250
New Zealand	16,130	40,750	-	56,880
South Africa	7,000	12,000	-	19,000
USA	58,480	189,955	14,290	262,725

Did you know…?

- In the First World War casualties for Britain and her allies were: dead: 9.6 million; wounded: 12.8 million.
- Forces casualties for Germany and her allies: dead: 8.0 million; wounded: 8.8 million
- British and her allies deaths were higher than the deaths of Germany and her allies.

Wounded British troops returning from the battlefield.

29

We will remember them

If you go to any of the war memorials on Armistice Day, or the Sunday nearest to it – at the 11th hour of the 11th day of the 11th month of any year – you will find people gathered there, holding wreaths made of poppies. There will be people holding flags belonging to the **Royal British Legion**.

Then, when the hour strikes, all these people, and people all over the country, will stop whatever they are doing. They will stop driving, stop working, stop learning. They will stand, or sit in complete silence for two minutes.

Then, in the silence, a distant cannon might be heard and a single bugler might blow a tune called the Last Post.

In the short service that follows, one of the readers will say these words:

"They shall grow not old, as we that are left grow old;
Age shall not weary them, nor the years condemn
At the going down of the sun and in the morning
We will remember them."

All of these memorials, the service of remembrance, the poem, the poppies on the wreaths, and the flags, are all part of our nation giving just a moment's thought to the terrible events of a war like no other before – and for all the wars since.

Did you know… ?

- There are war memorials in all Commonwealth countries, in France, in America and all other allied countries because they fought and lost men alongside the British.
- That there are war memorials in Germany because they lost dear ones, too.

Q **Why should we remember them?**

Glossary

Allies A group of countries who are on the same side and who work together in time of war.

Armistice An agreement to stop fighting. It usually comes before a peace treaty is signed.

bombardment A fierce and prolonged attack on an opposing force using shells or bombs dropped from aircraft which is designed to break the will of the opposition, destroy their guns, roads and so on. A bombardment usually comes before an attack using troops.

British Empire The territories ruled directly by the British king or queen.

gangrene A very nasty illness in which the cells of the body that have been infected with a disease begin to die due to lack of blood supply. Gangrene can often only be dealt with by amputation.

mine An explosive buried in a shallow pit in the soil and covered over to make it invisible. A small detonator sticks up from the mine. When pressure (foot or car tyre, for example) presses on the detonator, the mine is triggered.

Royal British Legion The United Kingdom's leading charity providing money and help to millions who have served, or who are currently serving in the British Armed Forces, and their dependents.

stalemate A situation in which both sides are evenly matched and no-one can win.

Index

Curriculum Visions

Curriculum Visions Explorers
This series provides straightforward introductions to key worlds and ideas.

You might also be interested in
Our slightly more detailed book, 'The First World War' and Teacher support materials.

Dedicated Web Site
Much more in detail can be found at:
www.curriculumvisions.com
(Subscription required)

A CVP Book
Copyright © 2010 Atlantic Europe Publishing

The right of Brian Knapp to be identified as the author of this work has been asserted by him in accordance with the Copyright, Designs and Patents Act 1988.

All rights reserved. No part of this publication may be reproduced, stored in a retrieval system, or transmitted in any form or by any means, electronic, mechanical, photocopying, recording or otherwise, without prior permission of the copyright holder.

Author
Brian Knapp, BSc, PhD

Senior Designer
Adele Humphries, BA

Editor
Gillian Gatehouse

Photographs
The Earthscape Picture Library, except *The Imperial War Museum* p4 (soldier), 16–17, 20–21, 22–23, 23c, 24c, 24–25, 28–29; *ShutterStock* cover.

Designed and produced by
Atlantic Europe Publishing

Printed in China by
WKT Company Ltd

Exploring Remembrance Day
– Curriculum Visions
A CIP record for this book is available from the British Library
ISBN 978 1 86214 670 9

This product is manufactured from sustainable managed forests. For every tree cut down at least one more is planted.